Knox County Murder Stories:
True Crime Stories From Knox County, Indiana

Table of Contents

Knox County Murder Stories:
True Crime Stories From Knox County, Indiana

Introduction

The naive, happy innocence of a child before it is ripped away.

That is what the killers profiled in this book have stolen from their victims. Their youth, their innocence, any happiness and normalcy associated with growing up in a world they thought they'd be safe in.

True crime isn't only about serial killers and rapists and pedophiles and organized crime. It is also about the victims left behind to serve their own life sentence, often times without anyone to help them make it through the awful ordeal.

These types of experiences was I'm sure enough to make one question their faith In God. Crimes like these – unexpected, violent, and forever – are hard enough to bear without the fact that the victim's killer has yet to be brought to justice. The feelings you would have to endure – anger, denial, disbelief, social withdrawl, and then even guilt, must have made the victim's survivors feel as though they were almost powerless over their own destiny.

One question does come to mind in the midst of all this horror and heartache, as the victim's family members face the accused in court: Were the perpetrators victims of parental abuse themselves as children?

Not that it would give them any excuse for their actions, but it might just go a long way in understanding the origins, and therefore the motives behind their crimes.

Ted Bundy, one of the prolific serial killers in history {and the man who literally coined the term 'serial killer'} in one of his last in depth interviews, just hours before his execution, warned of the long lasting and possibly deadly ramifications that can be associated with prolonged exposure to parental and sexual abuse as well as pornography:

The most damaging kind of pornography - and I'm talking from hard, real, personal experience - is that that involves violence and sexual violence. The wedding of those two forces - as I know only too well - brings about behavior that is too terrible to describe.

Although he used hard-core porn as a prime example, he did not necessarily condone his actions, using them as an excuse for his terrible crimes:

Before we go any further, it is important to me that people believe what I'm saying. I'm not blaming pornography. I'm not saying it caused me to go out and do certain things. I take full responsibility for all the things that I've done. That's not the question here. The issue is how this kind of literature contributed and helped mold and shape the kinds of violent behavior.

Regardless of the fact of whether they had an abusive childhood, one fact remains the same in the end. The young men and women who were victims of their crimes are now gone forever – except in the hearts and minds of their surviving family members, who must now begin their own healing process, if there even is such a thing under these circumstances. I myself believe that the human heart and mind is capable of healing itself with time – but will never forget *why* they are here

in this deep, dark place to begin with.
	God bless them and God speed their recovery.

David Boyer / September, 2023

Shine on, You Crazy Diamond
– the Brook Baker Case

"Remember when you were young, you shone like the sun.
Shine on you crazy diamond.
Now there's a look in your eyes, like black holes in the sky.
Shine on you crazy diamond."

Pink Floyd, 'Shine on You Crazy Diamond'

\#

The autumn wind of an Indiana night blows across the cemetery. It plays a malevolent, whistling tune through the trees of the cemetery as Tom Jones stands motionless, surveying the soft, brown earth that holds his 19-year-old granddaughter, Brook Baker. Tears well up in his eyes as he gazes down upon the inscription on her gravestone: ***Shine on you crazy diamond***.

Tom wipes the tears from his eyes and swallows the lump in his throat as he steps closer, touching the grave stone, stroking it gently with his fingers. "I miss you, little diamond," he says.

He comes here a lot now, reminiscing over all the good times he had with Brook, and their private conversations. One in particular comes to mind now, one that revealed the depth of her humanity and warmth at such a young age; *the naïve innocent happiness of a teenager before it was ripped away.*

The conversation running through his mind right now had gone like this; he and Brook had been sitting on the back porch sipping lemonade and watching the sunset. Right out of the blue, she'd asked, "Gramps, what's your view on the death penalty?" she'd asked him, right out of the blue. Brook was usually so laid back it had caught him off guard.

"Why do you ask that?" he'd said, sipping his lemonade.

She had looked out at the oncoming sunset with tears welling up in her eyes, swallowed a lump in her throat, and told him why. "It seems so unfair, that's all. You know; the way that murderers are either never caught or given short sentences. It's *not fair.*"

Her ambition of being a journalist was already shining through. "That's a tough question for me to answer; but no one has the right to take someone else's life except God." he'd told her, and to his own surprise, he'd meant it, too. *Then,* of course. Much later, his opinion had changed dramatically.

"Even if *they* kill somebody?" she'd said, apparently just as surprised at his answer. "And even if that somebody was *grandma*?"

Now *there* was a tough one to answer; how could he possibly tell his own granddaughter that it wouldn't be right to take the life of the man who'd taken the life of her grandmother? He wasn't even sure if *he* believed it. "Some people believe it just serves to create more misery," he said, "And more misery and death and more people serving life sentences for the rest of *their* lives."

Now, he arranges the days and moments of his life in an order he'll never recognize. Most of what God does in his life is behind the scenes stuff and the only proof of it is in those fingerprints. But he'll only find them if he's *looking* for them.

What it comes down to for the survivors is that it's not about them. It's about *Him* – and Brook's memory. Often people want to be the center of their own little universe and assume that it all revolves around them.

This is Brook's story, and how her world – although it has been physically silenced forever – still revolves and shines down upon the survivors every day.

#

September 7, 1997 – night.

It was no different than any other night at 216 Harrison Street, where VU student Brook Baker occupied an off-campus home.

Tired from a long day at school – and tired from the VU police ignoring her pleas for help from being harassed on campus by fellow students – she had decided to go to bed early. Tonight she was day dreaming again. Day dreaming about the cute guy she'd met yesterday at an off campus party. She didn't make a habit of attending dorm parties anymore; she didn't want to jeopardize her journalism career.

Just a few hours later she wakes up early, climbing out of bed sluggishly, hits the shower first, needing desperately to wake up. It's not that she dreads her dreams, thinking of him, but with each passing day, with each new dream, she finds herself becoming more distant, more confused, and soon surely her job performance at the lab will begin to suffer. She can't have that, *oh no*.

As she enters the bedroom, she notices the window is open. She doesn't remember leaving it open before she climbed in the shower, but shrugs it off and begins rummaging through her closet for something to wear to class.

With her back turned away from the rest of the room, she didn't see or hear Brian Jones as he stepped out of the shadows and grabbed her around the throat before she had time to scream.

Then fantasy became reality for him.

#

After not hearing from his sister for several days, Braun Baker became worried about her welfare and dropped by to check on her, finding her nude, lifeless body lying on the floor of her bedroom.

She had been sexually assaulted, strangled, and stabbed numerous times with a kitchen knife, which was found soaking in soapy water in the kitchen sink.

Stumped for clues at first, authorities soon began to suspect some young male students from a local fraternity, who had made threats against Brook after she had written an article about a recent {alleged} date rape at the fraternity. After questioning the young men, though, police eliminated them as suspects.

The next suspect was her own landlord, who would make a habit of walking in without knocking, on one occasion as she was just getting out of the shower. He too was soon eliminated as a suspect as well. A third theory was that a person posing as potential roommate killed her, because just days before her death, she had placed an ad in the campus newspaper looking for a roommate.

Meanwhile, police examined the physical

evidence, and tested DNA samples found on her with more than 50 suspects, but none of them matched.

Then in July of 1999, investigators searched the apartment of missing Vincennes college student Erika Elaine Norman, and were shocked to discover a nearly identical crime scene to Brook's crime scene, including the water running from the bathroom sink.

However, since her body was not found at the scene, she was still classified as missing. Soon, however, a young man named Brian Jones was brought in for questioning, after police learned that he was last seen with Erika right before her disappearance, and he was the former roommate of a man who had briefly dated Brook Baker.

He provided police with a DNA sample, and it matched the DNA found at the Brook Baker crime scene. He was arrested and charged with murder. Two weeks later, when the body of Erika Norman was found, he pleaded guilty to her murder, and in exchange for his plea, the death penalty was, unfortunately, off the table.

In his confession, he told police that he had thought about killing for a long time, even fantasized about it, and the 1996 film, *Curdled*, was the 'inspiration' for the method he used to kill Brook, as well as his love for Ted Bundy's methods of picking up women.

Maybe if someone – his family, or a close friend – had intervened soon enough on his behalf, got him treatment for his mental problems, Brook would still be alive today.

Then again, maybe not.

Most likely he would have continued to kill regardless of any intervention or treatment. His hero,

Ted Bundy, in the last interview with him before his execution, had this to say when asked if he thought some type of treatment would have been beneficial for him:

What I hope will come of our discussion is that I think society deserves to be protected from itself. As we have been talking, there are forces at loose in this country, especially this kind of violent pornography, where, on one hand, well-meaning people will condemn the behavior of a Ted Bundy while they're walking past a magazine rack full of the very kinds of things that send young kids down the road to being Ted Bundys. That's the irony. Treatment for this type of "disorder"? To what end? What's the point of locking someone up and pumping them full of drugs and carrying on with a lot of pointless conversations? The only REAL cure for this is either imprisonment or DEATH.

After examing all the source material I could find on Brian Jones, I'd say that his hero was right. I sincerely believe that if Jones hadn't been captured, with or without "treatment," he would have killed again.

For Jones, just like Bundy, he had already crossed the line between fantasy and reality, and, after spending some "quality" time there, had decided there was *NO* going back.

As for Brook, shine on, crazy diamond, shine on.

Brook's gravesite located in Wheatland, Indiana.
Shine on, crazy diamond.

Anti-Gay Hate Crimes Are Nothing New — the Mysterious Death of Brent Brand

It starts with a thrumming in the young man's ears, a sound very much like the thick, coursing current of a river swelling its' banks. Gradually he becomes aware that the frantic pulse is not water, but blood rushing through his veins, echoing in the pitch- black cavern of his inner ear.

The deafening thunder grows louder, terror wrapping its icy fingers around his pounding heart until he fears he may drown in his own blood. Louder, and fiercer, it doubles, and triples in intensity.

Abruptly, all falls silent.

Except for the laughter of the person dumping him in a ditch like a piece of discarded trash.

Still entombed in darkness, he gasps for breath, but instead of fresh air he swallows dirt, cutting off his air supply altogether now.

And then it starts.

A scream pierces him to the core.

And then another. Another.

His own screaming as he knows he is smothering to death.

And in the distance, but still audible, the laughter again, then retreating footsteps on black top, a car engine, then slowly but surely the awful silence again as the sound of the car engine fades into the darkness as well.

Then, mercifully, he lapses into unconsciousness and welcomes the inevitable, finding some comfort in the fact that he will be with God soon.

#

Were those what the last few moments of Brent's life really like? Based on his autopsy, most likely so.

In the Spring of 1986, as the Midwest was thawing out from a long cold Winter, a young, handsome, teenager named Brent Brand – so happy and full of love and life and hopes for the future – was found dead in a drainage ditch in Southern Illinois.

It was more than ten years before a young gay man, Matthew Shepard, was found tied to a fence and murdered. In the years that followed, Shepard became the poster boy, the ultimate symbol of the horrible violence and death associated with gay-bashing.

But in the case of Brent Brand, whose case ended up making national headlines as time went on, the case seemed, at first, as though it was going to be swept under the proverbial rug.

Th facts in the case were at first hazy at best. On the evening of May 9th, 1986, 18-year-old Brent returned home from a party momentarily to grab a pair of cutoff jeans. His Mother, Priscilla Wissel, said she was sitting in her rocking chair watching TV when Brent came home. She told him to call her and let her know what time he was coming home, or where he was staying if he spent the night somewhere, and he assured her he would.

She never saw him again.

Nine days later, his decomposed body was found in a drainage ditch by two boys riding three wheelers near Lake Lawrence, Illinois. He had been dumped off like a piece of trash and left to die – if he wasn't dead already.

One of the young men attending the party – which was mostly attended by homosexual men, if that should have had any significance – Jim Leyendecker, stated to police that on the night in question, he found Brand "unresponsive," at the party, and, in order to prevent himself or anyone else present at the party being blamed for Brand's death, took it upon himself to remove the body from the residence at 15 East St Clair in Vincennes, Indiana, and dumped it three miles away in Illinois, apparently in the belief that even if the body was found, the police wouldn't be able to make any connection.

He was wrong.

Such a "high profile" homosexual event – with local "celebrities" in attendance, one of which was long-time TV weatherman Kerry Dean – attracted the attention of the local authorities almost immediately.

Leyendecker, of Jeffersontown, Kentucky, was arrested and charged with a misdemeanor – moving a dead body and failure to report doing so – but was bailed out by his mother on a $500 cash bond shortly thereafter.

At the time, Knox County prosecutor Jerry McGaughey tried to light a fire under the ass of all involved, because despite the obvious circumstances surrounding Brand's death, the case seemed to be going nowhere fast.

Which had been great news for Brand's mother, Priscilla. She had long since had her suspicions about Leyendecker's involvement in her son's death. If he was innocent in any wrong-doing in Brand's death, why not just call the police or an ambulance upon finding the young man unresponsive? If it was a drug or alcohol overdose, why not do the right thing and try to save the young man's life? Did Brent Brand end up dying in a ditch just to cover up the fact that there were large amounts of alcohol and illegal drugs present at a party attended by TV and Vincennes University 'royalty'? ?

Or...was Brand still *alive* when Leyendecker moved the body – and he *knew* it - which would make him a *murderer*? Was Leyendecker only *pretending* to be gay, in order to gain Brand's trust, so he could slip him a lethal dose of drugs? Was Leyendecker actually a gay basher turned fledgling serial killer?

One of the tenants hosting the party, Steve Taylor, testified that during the course of the evening, Brand had been "locked up" in an upstairs room with Leyendecker for over two hours. When questioned about it, Leyendecker said all they did in the room was 'talk." If all they were doing was talking, why was the door locked – as if preventing Brand from escaping?

Steve Taylor and another friend, Shawn Carey, both testified that on the night in question, when Brand and Leyendecker finally emerged from the room, Brand, who'd been wearing cutoff jeans, was now clad in full length jeans and shirtless, as if he'd had a reason to change his attire while locked up in the room.

Taylor and Carey also testified that when Brand went into the room, he looked fine. When he emerged more than two hours later, he looked "woozy," and unstable, not coherent at all.

Steve said he asked Brand if he felt okay, and Brand said, "Yeah...I'm fine," but then almost stumbled down the stairs. Brand then turned to Leyendecker and asked if he could go back to the room and get his shirt, and Leyendecker seemed irritated, and said, "Don't worry, we can get it in the morning."

But for Brent Brand, morning never came.

#

The next morning, around 8 AM, Mrs. Wissel woke to find that Brent still hadn't returned.

Pacing back and forth nervously, she received a call from Steve Taylor around 11 AM, asking if Brent had made it home yet. She told Taylor, "Up? He's not even home yet." To which Taylor replied, "Oh my God."

When she asked him why he reacted that way, he told her that Brent was "sent home, by the way of back alleys and such, *very* intoxicated, around 2:30 AM."

Later, however, Taylor denied telling Mrs. Wissel that Brent had been intoxicated, and even went as far as to state that he did not see Brent drink anything at all at the party.

For the better part of the next week, Mrs. Wissel and other family members and friends searched in vain to find Brent, and had to learn about the discovery of his body one night while watching a local TV news station. When Brent was found, he was clad in the jeans he'd left home in, the shirt he'd left behind in the upstairs room, as well as the cutoff jeans. Also wrapped around his neck were a lot of cheap, gold chains that his own mother didn't even recognize. She stated that Brent never wore more than *one* chain at a time, either, which she also found very suspicious.

Illinois pathologist Dr Richard Peach said that the initial autopsy revealed that there were no drugs in Brent's system, and his alcohol level was "well below the legal limit for intoxication." If this is true, then why did Taylor and Carey claim he was "woozy," and incoherent, and he had left the party "staggering" through back alleyways to get home?

Leyendecker later changed his account of the events yet *again*, claiming that he saw Brent and other young men sniffing amyl nitrate, which is often used by the gay community to heighten orgasm. Dr Peach said the drug would be impossible to detect after death, because it completely dissipates after decomposition begins. But, he noted, it would be fatal if *swallowed*.

Leyendecker claimed he didn't see Brent using the drug, while Taylor, in a change of tune, claimed the drug was not present at the party at all.

By October of 1986, Detective Larry Eck and other authorities stopped their investigation altogether, claiming that after interviewing those at the party, he found no reason to take the investigation any further.

Mrs. Wissel remained heartbroken and dismayed at what she felt was a complete lack of interest in her son's death, as well as feeling deep down that there been a "cover-up" in the case. To this day, she feels that the only reason her son is dead is because he fell in with the wrong crowd – which, of course, was no reason for him to die under mysterious circumstances.

She said all she wanted now was to know what *really* happened to her son, and for him to have some justice for his wrongful death. Unfortunately, that was something that never happened.

As of this writing, the case still remains unsolved.

If It Could Happen Here, It Could Happen Anywhere
— the Murder of Lisa McCracken

Lisa sat frozen in fear, her captor sitting right across from her, holding a large kitchen knife.

He sat staring at his reflection in the blade, in the moonlight streaming through the window nearby. He looked up at Lisa and said, "You think I'm crazy, don't you?"

She didn't know what to say. She didn't want to agitate him, provoke any violent response. Swallowing a lump in her throat, she said, "I never said you were crazy. I don't even know you."

He seemed to calm down a bit, even cracked a smile. He said, "Let me clue you in on something. There is more than one term to describe someone who people think is crazy. Psychopath: They are very much in touch with reality, and despite their inability to feel empathy, guilt, or remorse, still have their shit together as far as knowing what it is they were sent here to do. Psychotic: Now, these are the dangerous ones, folks; they are completely out of touch with reality, and are delusional in the way they think they are God-like creatures, and/or there are monsters or bad people out to get them. I don't see any connection to myself in either category, actually."

Trying to gain his trust, to pacify him, she said, I don't think you are crazy. I just think you need help – I mean, someone to talk to."

That was the wrong thing to say to Jeffrey Whipps. He just knew he wasn't crazy, and he didn't need anyone to carry on boring, idle conversation with. What he wanted – he needed – was to kill someone. He wanted to watch them die and burn.

He stood up, brandishing the knife for emphasis. He said, "You just don't understand, do you?" He moved closer, and Lisa cowered in fear, pulling her knees up to her chest. "It's okay, though. You will understand soon enough, and so will everyone else."

Before Lisa could respond, buy some more time, he was upon her, driving the blade in deep. She began screaming in pain and agony, but her screams were quickly muffled by the blade as well.

Nearby, a neighbor had actually overheard someone {McCracken} screaming, but didn't bother to call the police.

#

Vincennes was once known by most people in the Tri-state area as the town where murder cases were very rarely solved, but in later years, things had begun to change for the better.

In the case of the Lisa McCracken murder, the killer, Jeffrey Allan Whipps, hadn't counted on the introduction of DNA evidence technology into modern law enforcement crime solving techniques.

By the late 90s, DNA evidence technology had begun to solve countless unsolved rape and murder cases – including the rape-murder of Lisa McCracken.

Still, her Mother, the Reverend Diane McCracken, couldn't help but still feel bitter about the way her daughter's case was handled – or mishandled – at the time of her daughter's death. In a press statement from 1987, she made her opinion of the way the Vincennes PD handled the investigation all too clear. "They were way too inexperienced to handle it correctly," she said, bitterly. "From the very moment my daughter died, things were not handled properly. When my husband visited the crime scene they were all sorts of people there, even students. They should *not* have been there. It *tainted* the crime scene."

The murder remained unsolved for thirteen years.

Then in 2000, a random DNA test uncovered new evidence linking Whipps to the murder of Lisa McCracken in 1987. Whipps was already serving an 89 year sentence for the 1995 murder of Vincennes resident Jill Slater. Slater was only 15 years old at the time of her death. He raped her, stabbed her, then set the apartment on fire, regardless of the fact there was an infant in the apartment Slater had been babysitting for.

The following day, the police contacted Whipps and asked to speak to him about an ongoing case. Thinking he had nothing to fear because of setting the fire, he agreed. Whipps came outside and sat in the back seat of the police car and began speaking with the officers when one of them noticed that Whipps left shoe had been burned. The officer asked Whipps if he could make a sketch of his shoe, to which Whipps agreed.

While sketching the shoe, the officer also noticed a blood stain on the shoe. At that point the officer informed Whipps he was under arrest and read him his Miranda rights.

Now with 40 years for the McCracken murder tacked on to his original sentence, the soonest he could be eligible for parole would be the year 2059.

He would be 90 years old.

Good riddance to bad rubbish, I say.

Hopes And Dreams Ripped Away
— The Killing Of Jill Slater

As radio celebrity Paul Harvey once said, "If you want to get away with murder, just go to Knox County, Indiana."

This outlook has changed a lot over the years, but in 1995, the outlook was still bleak at best.

Vincennes, Indiana residents, still reeling from the 1987 unsolved murder of VU student Lisa McCracken, were, in June of 1995, subjected to yet another nightmarish murder in our own community.

And, the same man was guilty of *both* murders.

#

Early on Father's Day morning of June 18th, 1995, killer Jeffrey Allen Whipps entered a home in which fifteen year old Vincennes resident Jill Slater was babysitting for a small child. Upon finding both Slater and the child sound asleep, he overpowered Slater, sexually assaulted her, killed her with a deep stab wound to the chest, then proceeded to set the house on fire, in order to burn up any evidence of the crime.

Then, in a real life travesty of justice, and although Whipps had already been a suspect in other local crimes, he was questioned by police, and then "cleared" of any involvment. Instead, local authorities concentrated on local resident Gilbert "Gib" Daughtery, and one of his known acquaintances, Wayne Swick, as suspects in the crime.

Daughtery had been her landlord at the time, which, as far as the police were concerned, gave him ample opportunity to be involved, have a legitimate reason for hanging around.

It was rumored that Swick was even detained at one time for questioning, but was eventually cleared of any involvment.

The police had even questioned Jill's boyfriend at the time, and, at one point, had even insinuated that possibly Jill had been dating Whipps, which was disgusting and absurd.

During the course of all of this nonsense, Whipps was still free to walk the streets.

But not for long.

#

At the time, the authorities were so absorbed in their own theories on the case, they almost let Whipps go free to commit other heinous crimes, but, luckily, the police felt compelled to question Whipps one more time.

They called his mother's residence, where he was living at the time, and asked to speak to him in person one more time. He reluctantly agreed, and upon arriving at his mother's home to speak with him, one of the officers noticed a burnt spot on his shoe, and what appeared to be a tiny blood stain.

He told Whipps he would like to sketch the sole of his shoe. Whipps removed the shoe and handed it to the officer.

While sketching, the officer noticed what he thought was blood on the shoe. He handed it to his superior officer. After examining it, the senior officer stopped the interview and said it was time to read Whipps his Miranda rights.

Whipps became extremely nervous, and there was brief tussle over the shoe, but the officers retained custody of it.

In the end, DNA evidence, although still partially in it's infancy at the time, connected Whipps to both the McCracken and Slater killings, and, in the Slater case, was found guilty of guilty of murder; arson, a class B felony; and sexual misconduct with a minor, a class C felony. The trial court sentenced him to eighty-nine years in prison.

But, the ordeal for the families of both victims was just beginning – all over again.

#

I have never really been sure what the word, "closure" actually means. I doubt that Jill's mother, Jane Manthe, has found it yet, either.

Even if the guilty party recieves life in prison, the survivors of the crimes never really find justice in the case. They, themselves, still have to serve a life sentence of their own. Crimes like these are unexpected, violent, and the memeories last *forever.*

The survivors are plagued with nightmares, guilt, and wondered why they couldn't have been there to hold their loved one's hand as they died. Their memory palace is filled with nightmarish vsions of their loved one's death. It's never really *over* for them.

They will be living their life sentence *forever* – and in much worse way than the killer ever will.

God speed them in their recovery, and may God bless the victims and keep them close. Amen.

Blood Isn't Really Thicker Than Water
— The Murders Of Darrell and Marjorie McKendree

August 8, 2001, Vincennes, Indiana.

Vincennes, Indiana resident James Hitt was asleep in his home when a loud knock on the door startled him awake around 2:45 am. Upon answering the door, he found nineteen-year-old Jeremy Vennard standing there, his eyes wild and crazy, and wearing a pair of bloody socks on his hands.

When Hitt asked Vennard what happened, Vennard stated that he had just killed his father, Darrell McKendree, and his stepmother, Marjorie, by "slashing their fucking throats," and then robbing them.

Then to prove the fact, Vennard produced some bloody dollar bills, a small bag of marijuana, and a pack of Marlboro cigarettes from his pants pocket. At that point Hitt and Vennard walked back to the McKendree's home to see if they were still alive, stopping long enough to pick up another acquaintance, Tom King, before going there.

Upon their arrival at the McKendree residence, Hitt and King could see the McKendree's lifeless bodies lying on the living room floor in a pool of blood. The scene was at the least horrific: both victims had their throats slit multiple times with a knife. In addition to the neck wounds, both victims had a knife jammed into one of their eyes, and one of Marjorie's ears had been cut off and stuffed into her mouth.

One of the men who'd accompanied Vennard to the residence immediately left to call 911.

Upon their arrival at the crime scene, local police officer James Dotson noticed an empty wallet lying next to Darrell's body, his back pocket had been ripped, his front pocket lining was turned inside out, and a marijuana pipe, knife, and package of Marlboro cigarettes were on the floor, indicating a robbery as well as a double murder.

It was also established that the majority of the stab wounds were inflicted "post-mortem," including the injuries to the victims' eyes, indicating that Vennard had, in an act of horrible cruelty, hadn't found slitting their throats satisfactory enough for him, and had felt compelled to inflict more insult to injury by maiming their corpse.

At his sentence hearing in April of 2003, Vennard showed no remorse for his actions whatsoever. He was sentenced to 130 years in prison.

#

What has always remained a complete mystery was Vennard's reasoning behind his actions.

A close family member of the victims, Roberta Marie {Brewer} McKendree, has informed me that both Darrell and Marjorie were loved and respected by their family and friends, and had a strong family ethic, both of hard working and devoted to the normal family atmosphere.

Darrell was a good hearted man, who would go as far as to drive all the way to check on his mother, Dorothy, to make sure she was okay and had all she needed. Marjorie was a good woman as well, a devoted wife and mother and enjoyed normal, fun activities such as going to Bingo, but otherwise a homebody and happy to be one.

Which begs the question...why would Jeremy harbor such hatred and loathing toward them he would go as far as commit cold blooded murder?

Was it a case of personal jealousy against his stepmother? Did he feel she had tried to take the place of his real mother? Was it hatred toward his father for allowing her into the family fold?

Could it have been psychosis brought on by drug and-or alcohol abuse? Or a combination of both jealousy-hatred and substance abuse that made him snap, finally teeter over the edge of sanity?

Regardless of what his reasoning or motive was behind the murders, one fact remains the same; he took the lives of two innocent people – and family members, no less – and this case, justice was served, and he has been made to pay for his crimes.

Unfortunately, though, the rest of Darrell and Marjorie's surviving family members have been left behind to serve their own life sentence, who must now begin their own healing process, if there even is such a thing under these circumstances.

I myself believe that the human heart and mind is capable of healing itself with time – but will never forget *why* they are here in this deep, dark place to begin with.

God bless them and God speed their recovery.

Vanished In Vincennes
- The Mysterious Disappearance and Death of Dolores Oliver

Introduction:

The Northern side of Vincennes, known infamously as "the North end," in the 1970s, was, at one point, a melting pot of crime.

Drugs, alcohol, burglary, arson, street fighting, and bar brawling was the norm on any given day. Residents were in fear of their safety after dark – and at times even during the daytime hours. In the North end you either belonged or you didn't and if you didn't, you didn't come in unless you got your ass whipped.

Street toughs ruled their corner of the block, and dared any "outsider" to cross their turf. A trip to the store for a loaf of bread was considered an act of bravery. But regardless of the area's well deserved reputation, there were families that lived within the community, that, regardless of their so called "tough reputation," were in reality no more dangerous than we would consider ourselves to be.

So was the Oliver family. Raymond Oliver was a hard working man doing his best to provide for his wife and seven children in a tough part of town, which made it even harder to do so, with all the temptations of local crime and the party lifestyle so available to his kids.

Yet he persevered. His wife, Dolores, fondly nick-named 'Lert' by her friends as a term of endearment, was out an out-going and friendly woman who was well liked by all who knew her.

Yet, on September 7, 1974, while on a visit to a

local bar to chat with friends, she simply vanished without a trace. Foul play was immediately suspected by her family, who knew in their hearts that they could think of absolutely no one who would want to do her any harm.

Yet her lifeless body was found at the end of October in a bean field by a farmer in Illinois. Lawrence County coroner Dale Nichols was able to make a positive ID through dental records and a ring Mrs Oliver was wearing.

Vincennes Detective Leslie Chanley was assigned to the case, and that had seemed to be when the case went sour – and came to a complete standstill.

It is my hope that the information in this chapbook, examined from a point of view other than law enforcement and social media, will shed some light on the circumstances surrounding the case.

David Boyer / September, 2023

To have even a basic understanding of what may or may not have happened, let us establish a "time line," so to speak:

September 7, 1974 – early evening.

After a long day, Mrs Oliver decides to walk down to the local tavern, Burke's, {later known as The Third Base, not to be confused with the Imperial tavern} for drinks and friendly banter with some of the other bar patrons. It's just like any other September night, a typical Indiana twilight, clear, perfect, and breezy. As you walk along, enjoying the weather on your way to see your friends, you can smell pizza and hot-dogs in the air, and hear the sounds of neighborhood children playing nearby and the steady but quiet hum of traffic as it glides along Second Street, more hard working folks on their way home to eat dinner, shower, and then out to congregate with friends and family. This is *her* world: nothing fancy, but very important and endearing to her nonetheless.

As Mrs Oliver walks into the bar, all who know her turn to greet her with big smiles and friendly hugs, always glad to see her and feeling all the more blessed to be in her presence. Over the next few hours, friendly banter is exchanged, beer mugs are refilled, jokes are told and the music blaring from the ancient jukebox helps set the mood for the rest of the evening. Everyone knows everyone else here, and the overall mood is normally one of fun and celebration for the simple things in life, a festive atmosphere – unless a fight breaks out now and then, over a girlfriend or a pool game. Typical small town bar on a weekend. Then, at the end of the evening, apparently oblivious to everyone else, Mrs Dolores Oliver simply *vanishes*, and right under everyone's nose, in a terrifying turn of events that would last for an excruciating six weeks before her family and friends learned of her fate.

#

September 7th to October 25th, 1974

Over the next six, long, excruciating weeks, her family and friends could only sit back and wonder: Why didn't *anyone* see her leave the bar? And if so, why didn't they step forward with any crucial information, such as a description of the potential suspect? For some reason, the place where she had always felt safe was now full of people keeping their mouths shut and turning a blind eye to the recent disappearance of a beloved friend.

The nightmarish visions that went through their minds I am sure was a torturous punishment no family should have to endure. Where could she be? She wouldn't just take off with a friend or go out drinking and not contact her family.

It was rumored that at times, if she and her husband were not getting along, she would leave for a couple of days, but she would always come back unscathed. Otherwise, she was known to be a very good hearted woman, too, who would do almost anything to help a person in need. If you were hungry? She would gladly make you something to eat. Needed a place to stay? No problem, there's the couch.

It didn't take them long to realize and face up to the fact that foul play most definitely had to be involved.

But...*who* would want to hurt her? And *why?*

Yet, someone must have had what they *thought* was a reason to harm her. Her niece, Gaye Collins Dillon, told me the following heartbreaking story after visiting the murder site:

I remember going over to the cornfield you could see the outline of her body, pieces of her hair was in the mud, her finger nails where laying there , little pieces of her skirt was in the mud. She had laid there in muddy water for a while and they said the animals and the birds had got to her. It was horrible. Was she killed here and then dumped over there? WHY wasn't anyone trying to help us find out what happened?

Very good question.

Rayetta Mincey, Mrs Oliver's eldest daughter, had this to say:

When Mom first went missing, my dad and my brothers went everywhere to look for her , if any one thought they saw her. it didn't matter where, they would go, this went on the entire time she was missing. It was always a big let down when they would return from a sighting and didn't have any news, We always felt like the police were not doing anything and we all felt helpless. The not knowing was so hard, always wondering if she was hurt some where and couldn't get help or if she was being held against her will, the thoughts you have are horrible. None of us really knew what to do. But we all KNEW something was wrong.

Something was wrong, indeed.

Something *horribly* wrong.

Who else but her own, close-knit family would *know* that there had to be foul play involved? Why were their pleas for help or information ignored? Why wasn't her case given more consideration?

This is what her family had to endure for over six weeks - and beyond - without any results excepting for her ghastly, untimely death.

#

October 25ᵗʰ, 1974 – to present day.

There are many theories that have surrounded this case, one of which, I am sure, is that Mrs Oliver just simply ran away from home with another man, to escape the responsibility of her own home life, and her new boyfriend just happened to turn out to be a killer.

Another was that her husband was angry with her for something, and he did it in a fit of rage. {This is also very doubtful, because Raymond Oliver was known to have loved his wife very much, and never remarried after her death.}

In yet another, it was rumored that someone she knew from Illinois did it, {hence the body dump in Illinois} but that theory has never been proven either. In small town murder cases, rumors and gossip usually abound to no end, and now, with social networking web sites like Facebook available for gossip mongers to post their BS and drama, it's even worse.

I, myself, have already dismissed this theory

under the circumstances, after corresponding with her family. I realize that the police must always examine a murder case from all angles, in order to eliminate innocent people from the suspect list, but in this case, I just found it to be totally absurd.

Another theory the police always consider is that a murder victim could have been preyed upon by a drifter just passing through. In my own personal studies of serial killers, I have noticed that a lot of them are *drifters*, who live a nomadic lifestyle, who kill and then move on quickly, in order to elude capture.

Some even change there MO as well, shooting one victim, stabbing another, to throw the police off their trail and confuse them. Serial killer Henry Lee Lucas was known to have passed through Indiana in the early 70s upon his release from prison, too, but I have dismissed this theory because the timeline between her death and his release just didn't add up.

But with this case, I have my sincere doubts about the aforementioned theories, and have come up with my own.

I, myself, believe that it was someone who knew her *personally*, if only in passing, maybe a so called "friendly acquaintance," someone she would not suspect of any wrong doing, would have no motive to harm her, and that is how they got away with her murder. Someone she had a beer with now and then. Just another harmless, friendly face in the crowd.

Until just the right moment, when that friendly face suddenly turned into a mask of horror and malice, and it was too late to turn back.

I may be wrong, but I don't think so.

I have, in privacy and secrecy, conducted a lot of

research into this case, invested months of my time into trying to build a profile. My profile is as follows:

#

A male, 35 to 45 years old. {If still alive today, he would be around 75 to 80 years old, which means he would most likely be dead by now, or incarcerated for similar crimes. Most serial killers, unless imprisoned and or executed, eventually die from natural causes or terminal illness. Examples: Henry Lee Lucas, dead at age 65 from heart failure; Charles Manson, dead at 83 from terminal illness, both died while incarcerated.}

I think most of all he was a *loner*, most likely lived alone, and lived within walking distance or a very short drive to the bar where Mrs Oliver would congregate with friends. Although a loner, he would most likely "fit in" to the bar crowd, and have no trouble making friends if he chose to do so, and possess a simplistic but nonetheless uncanny ability to make women feel sorry for him, maybe even charm them into leaving with him out of pity.

He has kept this secret all these years, to himself, never telling a friend or bragging about it to anyone, therefore the terrible secret staying a secret that went to the grave with him.

Other possible characteristics and past history: childhood ritual abuse by one or both parents, including sexual abuse and beatings.

Other outstanding characteristics may include a propensity for alcoholism, a quick temper, physical violence, and a strong hatred and loathing for the opposite sex – including their own mother – that stems from a childhood trauma.

As a writer, I have a past history of immersing myself in the particular surroundings that I believe will benefit me in my research.

For example: in my research pertaining to alcoholism {I, myself, am a recovering alcoholic, 16 years sober now} I would go to a place, soak in its atmosphere, its nuance, and let it speak to me. I would sit in a rear corner booth in Bud's tavern, a known haunt, like many others, for the walking wounded when they are looking for love in all the wrong places Under the crimson glare of the bar's lights, I stare out at a sea of empty lives.

Men and women searching for the momentary distraction of drunken comradery to numb themselves from the pain of their own reality. The décor reeks of a pervasive hopelessness that has settled even into the Formica tables; an air of desperation as thick as the spent Scotch and stale beer fumes from the nearby tables and the odor of their famous chicken fills the kitchen area.

Believe it or not, it was there I found my greatest inspiration.

Just as I do when researching true crime cases: After conducting all my research, I try to immerse myself in the mind of the killer. Think like *they* would think. Place myself in *their* surroundings.

I imagine myself sitting among the walking wounded in a small bar in the North end of Vincennes, Indiana, in September of 1974, my eyes searching the crowd for that one "special lady."

Now, considering the fact I am not a *professional* true crime writer, mainly just a true crime "buff," I could be wrong about all of this.

But I don't think so.

In all honesty? I believe that if Dolores Oliver's killer is still alive today? He is still living in Vincennes, Indiana - or possibly incarcerated somewhere in Indiana for a similar crime - and still harboring his terrible secret, while her murder still remains unsolved.

To make matters even worse, there was no DNA technology back then, which means even if her remains were exhumed today, there would be no DNA evidence to speak of, after her body being prepared for burial by the funeral home attendant.

Therefore, as far as latent evidence is concerned, I guess we must hope and pray for a miracle here, hope someone comes forward with their own evidence to share, but that's highly unlikely.

Small town secrets tend to *stay* that way.

#

Overviews and final opinions:

In closing, let us take a moment to re-examine the case in it's entirety:

On September 7th, 1974, Mrs Dolores Oliver takes a leisurely stroll down to the local bar to congregate with friends, which was nothing out of the ordinary.

A few hours later, and with many potential witnesses in attendance, she simply vanishes without a trace.

For the next six weeks, her family and friends search for her in vain, with no new leads or any direct cooperation from the local authorities.

Over six weeks later, her body is found in a field in Illinois. {NOTE: this is the *FIFTH* Illinois body dump of an Indiana murder victim since 1974. It could very well be a coincidence, but who knows?}

The case is handed over to Vincennes Detective Leslie Chanley – and almost immediately goes cold. It is rumored that he had a past grudge against the family, therefore didn't bother to pursue the case with any certain amount of integrity or professionalism, allowing the case to grow cold before the investigation even got started.

Mrs Oliver's niece, Gaye Collins Dillon, upon traveling to Illinois to speak with the Lawrence County Sheriff about seeing pictures of her Aunt's remains, was told at first that the pictures were something she wouldn't want to see, then shortly thereafter was told that the evidence was "more or less" wasn't available.

If the case wasn't closed – hadn't even really been pursued yet – then why was the evidence discarded?

Why wasn't a place like a Sheriff's department equipped with storage space to accommodate the gathering of crucial evidence?

Where was the list of witnesses that saw her walk into the bar, but didn't see her leaving with anyone? Were some of the bar patrons themselves in on some type of cover-up? Protecting her killer for some reason? And were the local police in on the cover-up? If so, why?

Did she *know* her killer? Was it someone she had known for a long time and trusted? Was it a man who lived close by whom no one at the bar would never suspect? Was it a drifter just passing through?

Or...could my *own* theory be correct?

So many questions, and unfortunately, so few *real* answers. One fact remains the same: someone out there *KNOWS* what happened, and is keeping their mouth shut.

I think her killer, if not dead from natural causes or execution, is still out there, and hiding in plain sight.

He could be the nice old guy next door who lets you borrow his lawnmower and offers you a cold beer.

He could be your elderly Uncle's former ex-con cell mate who never had much to say and stays to himself unless it's to go to the liquor store for more alcohol to drink his inner demons away.

It is my sincere hope that after reading this, someone out there somewhere will remember something they heard or saw {or felt guilty about keeping a secret for all these years} and come forward, finally allowing her soul to rest in peace and her family to receive some long awaited and much needed closure.

Case photos:

Police Seek Leads In Oliver Case

Vincennes City, Lawrence County, Ill., and Illinois State Police are still investigating the death last fall of Delores Oliver of Vincennes but have 'completely run out of leads,'' Vincennes Police Major Les Chanley said Thursday.

Chanley said that because of the total dearth of new leads on the mysterious death of Mrs. Oliver, he once again is asking persons with any knowledge of the case to contact him. Chanley pledged he would keep all sources confidential.

Mrs. Oliver, a petite blonde who was the mother of seven children, disappeared last Sept. 7 after last being seen at Bert's Tavern near Portland and St. Clair streets. The 46-year-old wife of Raymond Oliver, 21 E. Portland Ave. remained missing for six weeks even after her family posted a reward for information leading to her discovery.

On Oct. 25 Mrs. Oliver's badly decomposed body was found in a soybean field about four miles east of Lawrenceville. An autopsy was performed but failed to turn up any bullet wounds or other signs of violence.

'The body was far too decomposed to come up with anything,'' Chanley said. Authorities said they suspected foul play because the body was found about 100 feet off Bus. 50.

Police, however, also reported that the field where Mrs. Oliver had been found had been under floodwater for about two weeks after heavy rains had drenched the area. This led to the speculation that the body could have drifted to the field from another site.

A Sun Commerical news clipping from October, 1974.

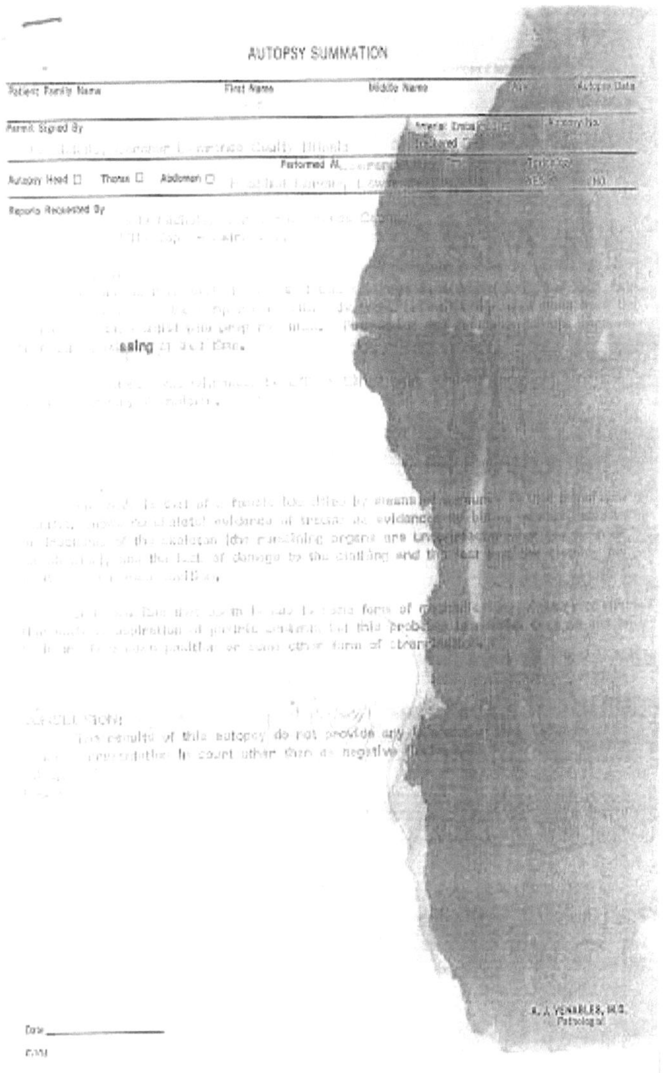

The autopsy report typed up by Dale Nichols. It is even less than conclusive, only providing a "possible" cause of death, which "may have been" strangulation. In my opinion, it either is or is not strangulation. The neck is one of the most vulnerable parts of the human body. Any coroner worth their salt can tell you the neck can be slashed, twisted, snapped, or held in a vise until the owner either passes out or asphyxiates.

You would not need an extensive knowledge of the human anatomy to know how to strangle someone. It either was or it wasn't the cause of death. Yet another inconsistency in the way the autopsy was performed and diagnosed.

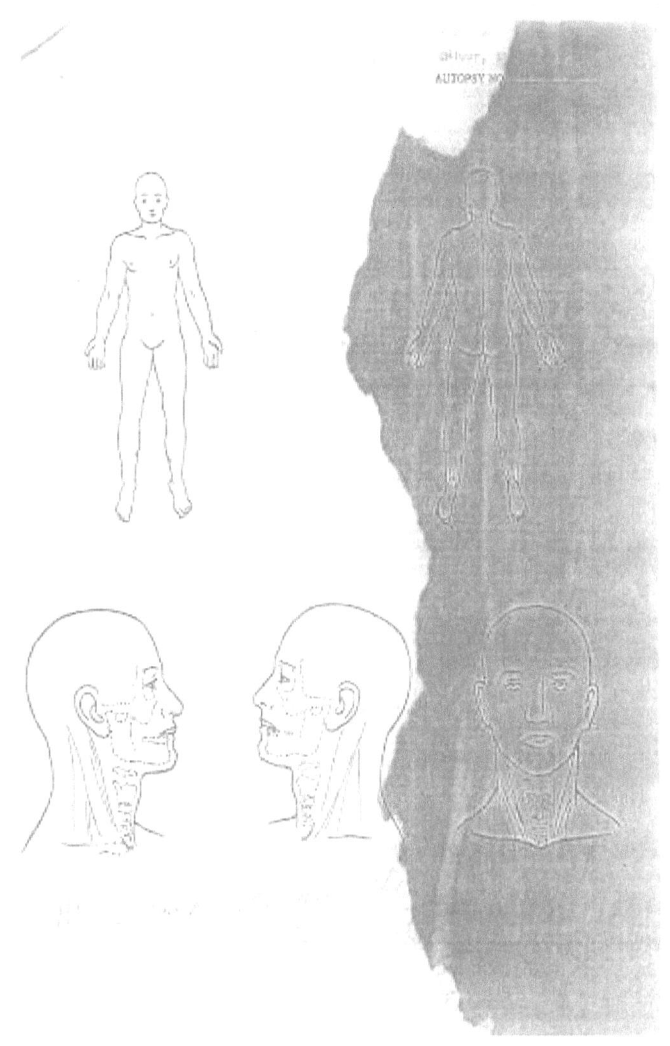

An autopsy diagram. As you can see, almost half the page, like the autopsy report, is blacked out by a stain of some type, making it almost unreadable. Was it just a coincidence, and "accident" on the coroner's part? Considering the other facts in the case up until that point, it's very doubtful.

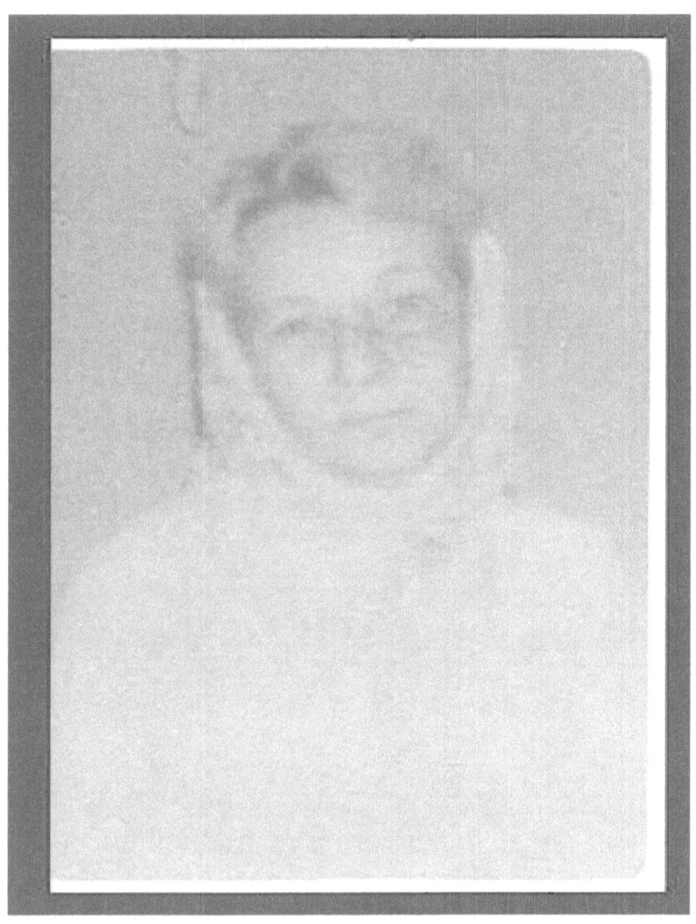

Dolores Oliver, known fondly by her friends as "Lert."
The exact date of the photograph is unknown.

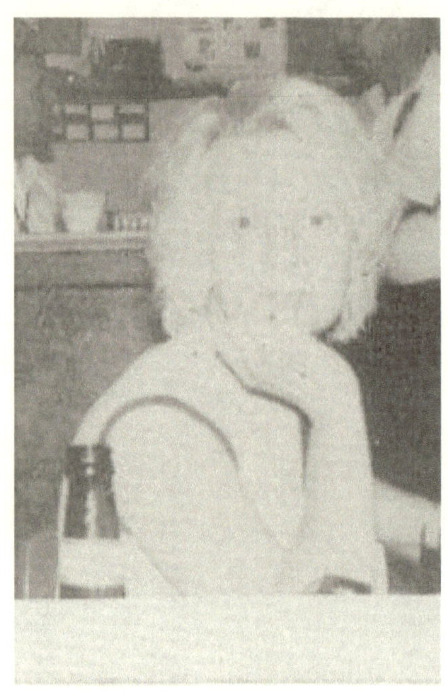

Dolores Oliver at the tavern she frequented before her death. Little did she know or would have ever been able to even fathom what horrors awaited her in the near future.

On the left: Burke's tavern on North Second Street in Vincennes, Indiana {later known as Third Base} was the last place Dolores Oliver was known to be seen alive and well. On her last night there, she simply vanished – and, mysteriously, nobody that was there that night heard or saw anything suspicious.

Dolores and Raymond's gravestone located at Memorial Park cemetery in Vincennes, Indiana.

The Legal System Failed Her:
– The Murder Of Allison Rinsch

Damon Catt was on his way to being a full fledged serial killer if it hadn't been for the fact he was just plain *dumb*.

A fledgling serial killer in his own right, Damon Catt had already done prison time for aggravated battery before he so cruelly murdered Allison Rinsch.

Like so many other killers who slip through the cracks in our justice system, Catt had quite the interesting history of violent behavior long before he met Allison, which was a crime in itself. More often than not these days, men like Catt – obviously a danger to themselves let alone anyone else – are constantly swallowed up by our legal system and spit back out just as quickly, to act out more violent crimes.

And unfortunately for Allison Rinsch, he was "in the mood" that day – and wielding a knife.

The scenario surrounding the murder of Allison Rinsch was one we've all heard too many times before, like a graphic, sexually charged, violence-laden soap opera a lot of us have watched on TV in the afternoon with nothing better to do with our time. A young woman, attractive and intelligent and has everything going for her, ignores her family's concerns – as well as the obvious signs her so called relationship is in big trouble – and eventually ends up paying the ultimate price.

Sad thing was, at the time of Allison's death, the police were just then learning more about Catt's history. The prosecutor's office says Catt had a current meth possession case pending in Knox County. Authorities say there had been reported battery charges in other jurisdictions. Catt had already served prison time for a battery conviction. Police say that case involved Catt attacking a police officer. Then why was he already out of prison?

Believe me, men like Catt know how to "work the system," and know how the system works. Men like Catt have been through the wringer so many times they know how to come out smelling like a rose garden.

It is, unfortunately, common knowledge that our legal system sometimes fails more than it succeeds when it comes to murderers. Whether it is prison overcrowding or getting released for "good behavior," a killer will always end up back on the street – and ready to kill again.

Prime example: serial killer Henry Lee Lucas committed his first murder at age 15. Since he was a minor, he got probation. At age 19, he killed his own mother. Time served? Less than 7 years – he was released for "good behavior."

From there, he went on to be one of the most infamous and prolific serial killers in American history.

Reason being? He knew how to *work the system*. Most serial killers, despite their outward appearance and general personality, can charm just about anyone into thinking they have been "rehabilitated."

In the case of Damon Catt, I believe he knew *exactly* what he was doing on November 19, 2007, when he proceeded to stab her to death, leaving her lying dead in a pool of her own blood.

Nevermind the fact that, in the past, he had been arrested for knocking her unconscious and pushing her out of a moving car.

Or the time he pulled a large, 38-inch sword on a police officer, threatening to kill him with it.

Or...the *multiple* domestic abuse calls made from Allison's home address, with Catt in attendance – as the perpetrator, of course.

He knew *exactly* what he was doing.

He was not "temporarily insane."

He *enjoyed* killing, so he did it. He loved the *power* he felt over Allison. The feeling of jamming the knife blade into her tiny, frail body as she most assuredly begged and pleaded for her life.

Allison's grandfather claimed that Catt was very vocal about his violent intentions toward her, but nobody would listen. He was, however, very thankful that her two-year-old son wasn't harmed.

Luckily, Rinsch's mother had been taking care him the afternoon of the murder.

Unluckily for Catt, he was sentenced to 63 years in prison for her murder. I think that was letting him off too easy. Contrary to whatever crazy excuse was going through his demented, Meth-fueled mind at the time, she didn't ask for it, to be so cruelly murdered in cold blood for just caring about someone.

I am curious as to how long it will take Catt to be released *this* time.

Damon Catt, murderer.
He knew how to beat the system.

Life Is Cheap
      – the Murder of Dallas Wallace

{No image available}

Dallas Wallace had a good score this morning.

He still had a stash left over from his monthly checks, and now, by the grace of God – or just drunk luck – he had just cashed in a big load of scrap metal for $103.50.

He felt on top of the world. Thanksgiving was right around the corner, and he had plenty of cash for a decent dinner and, of course, some good party favors.

After going to the grocery store and liquor store, he decided to drop by Bud Small's tavern to socialize for a while. The little tavern was a popular meeting place for neighborhood residents seeking some good company and some good laughs, and Dallas knew he was always welcome there.

After having a few cold beers and playing the tip-boards without any luck, he decided to count his blessings and keep what cash he had left intact – around $45.00 – and head home to have a bite to eat and take a nap. He had been on his feet all day, and needed to rest up for the upcoming holidays.

As he walked out of the tavern, bidding his friends farewell, little did the other patrons know it was the last time they would see Dallas alive.

Later that night, waiting in the shadows of the treeline in Pearl City, Indiana, were two young men who planned to rob Dallas of his good fortune – and instead ended up taking his life for no reason at all.

Although a heavy drinker and bootlegger with a reputation for being a tough character, Wallace was in fact a very personable fellow who didn't bother anyone. He was as harmless as a house fly unless heavily intoxicated and provoked.

On the night of November 22nd, 1994, Dallace Wallace, in a state of intoxication and unable to defend himself, was robbed – and shot in the head. He died for a grand total of $45.00.

I guess life really *is* cheap.

Pearl City, Indiana, at one time, was a small, run down community of ramshackle houses and derelict trailers nestled in between the town levee and the Wabash River basin. Although occupied by a somewhat diverse group of people, they all got along with each other, even helped each other when need be, and often watched out for their own.

And Dallas was no exception to the rule. Although a loner a great deal of the time, he otherwise was liked by his neighbors and anyone else who knew him, and when he was robbed and killed for $45.00, the small community of Pearl City – as well as a lot of the residents of Vincennes, Indiana, were outraged.

But justice for his murder was pretty swift. Not too long after his body was found, local residents Roger Coy, Jr and Milton Lane, Jr, were arrested and charged with his murder. According to a friend, Chris Hand, he dropped Coy and Lane off near Dallas' cabin late that night, for the purpose of robbing him of what they had anticipated would be a decent score. When he came back later to pick them up, Coy told Hand he had killed Dallas, and even showed him Dallas' wallet as proof.

In court, an estranged friend of Coy testified that Coy bragged about the robbery-murder, but still couldn't believe that he had "killed the old drunk for a lousy forty-five dollars."

It didn't take long for both of them to be found guilty.

The trial court imposed concurrent sentences of sixty years for murder and ten years for burglary for both Coy and Lane. If they happen to be unlucky enough to live that long, they will both could be around 70 years old upon their release.

Life was cheap to Coy and Lane, but they now have the rest of their lives to ponder just how *expensive* their actions really were.

Milton Lane being led away from the courthouse after his sentencing. He was given a sentence of 50 years, but was released in 2013, on good behavior, after serving 16 years. He is now a Christian, and serves to help other ex cons to cope with life after incarceration.

A newspaper article on Roger Coy. He too was given a stiff sentence, but was released in 2015, and whose whereabouts are unknown. Whether his incarceration changed his life for the better remains to be seen.

The Burning Barn
– The Murder of Sherry Gibson

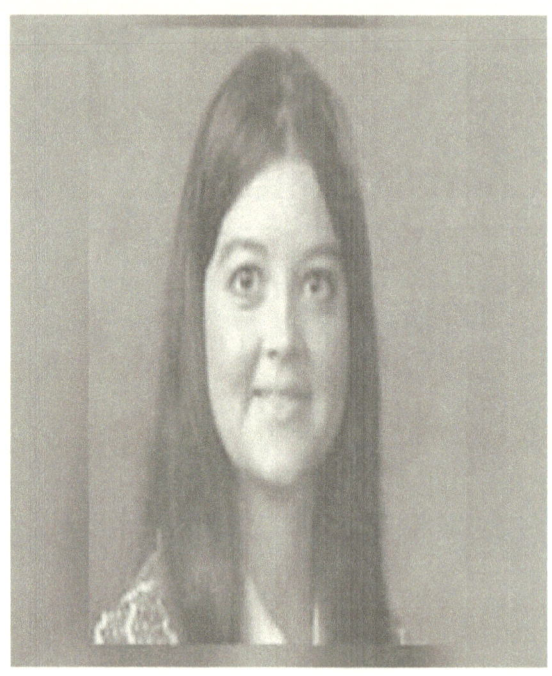

Monroe City area, Knox County Indiana
March 1st, 1975

Sherry opened her eyes to find herself in a old, weather-beaten barn-house. Her hands were tied behind her back and she was gagged. She shook slightly as a breeze came through the broken window. She looked down and saw that the person that had kidnapped her had removed her clothes, leaving her in her bra and underwear. As she looked up again, she saw her kidnapper coming back in from outside. His name was Wayne.

She knew his name because she'd heard it mentioned numerous times on the way to the barn, while she was lying in the back seat of a stranger's car. She'd heard a woman's voice too, but no name was mentioned.

What her captors had done with her boyfriend, Lindy, she did not know. But judging by her current situation, it might be better for her current frame of mind if she didn't know.

The man named Wayne was holding a bottle of cheap liquor. His eyes were bloodshot and wild and his face pale. He looked more like a ghost than a man.

She felt another shiver as he spoke to her in a deep, guttural tone of voice. "Are we comfy? I hope so, because we are going to have some fun."

Whatever type of 'fun' he was speaking of she could just imagine, but she tried her best to block it from her mind. Not that it would do her any good in the end.

"Where is my boyfriend?" she asked, thinking more of his welfare than her own. She'd decided she did want to know, no matter how hard it might be to hear about his fate.

Wayne just grinned and said, "No need to worry about him, babe. He's going to be just fine." He lit a cigarette and exhaled. "You should be more concerned with what I'm getting ready to do to you."

Knowing now that her fate was sealed as soon as woke up in the barn, she lost interest quickly in trying to pacify this creep. She said, "Over my dead body, you will."

He stepped closer, grinning again. He reached behind him and pulled a long, sharp knife from his belt. He said, "Well, that can be arranged.."

#

Were those what the last few moments of Sherry Gibson's life were *really* like? As a writer of both fiction and non-fiction, I'd say my theory, once again, was most likely mild in comparison.

But there was *nothing* mild about the way Wayne Gulley, and his ex-girlfriend, Ella Mae Dicks, so brutally murdered Gibson.

The horrific crimes had authorities and local residents alike dumbfounded as well as terrified for years, due to the brutal and vicious nature of the crimes. Gibson had been beaten and stabbed *dozens* of times and raped, the crime so brutal it made some of the Charles Manson murders of 1969 look almost tame in comparison. To add insult to injury, the barn was then set ablaze by Gibson's assailants, in hopes she'd burn up, therefore leaving no trace of evidence for police.

Since there was no DNA technology back then, the killer{s} got away with it – and seemed to vanish without a trace.

#

Gibson and her boyfriend, Lindy Alton, had been out riding around in his car, enjoying the beautiful early Spring weather when they'd decided to park along a rural road known as sort of a 'lover's lane' to local residents.

It wasn't too long after when they were accosted by Dicks and Gulley, who had been out 'joyriding,' who ordered Alton into the trunk of his vehicle and left him behind, while they placed Gibson into their own vehicle and drove her to a barn about seven miles away, where the crimes took place over the course of the next few horrifying hours.

The next morning, a local farmer found Alton's car and when he approached it, he could hear pounding from the trunk and Alton screaming for help. When the police arrived at the scene, they initially doubted Alton's story, because of the manner in which he spoke to them, and seemed very nervous talking about the incident, stuttering when he spoke to them.

What they didn't know at the time was, Alton had suffered a blow to the head as a child, leaving him with a speech impediment.

Before long, the police received a call to investigate a barn fire a few miles away, and upon arriving, unearthed Gibson's charred body from the barn, realizing that Alton had apparently been telling the truth.

An autopsy revealed that Sherry Lee Gibson had been savagely beaten, raped, and stabbed *dozens* of times. Three deep knife wounds to the heart officially caused her death.

Alton worked with a police sketch artist to describe the male and female attackers. He gave detailed specifics, down to the types of eyeglasses they wore, the part in the man's hair, and the specific location of a mole on the woman's face. These images would prove invaluable — but not until many years later.

#

As time went on, police had no new leads in the case whatsoever. Then, in August of 1977, police recieved a new lead in the case from an employee of the local juvenile hall about an inmate named John Jeffers, a youth who claimed he had valuable information about the Sherry Gibson murder.

Upon being questioned, Jeffers broke down in tears and said he and a friend, Kenneth Shaner, had committed the crime.

At the time, Shaner was serving in the United States Army and was stationed in Germany. He was immediately extradited back to Indiana to stand trial for his part in the crime.

However, when the two men went to trial, Jeffers recanted his testimony, stating that he fabricated the whole thing as a revenge tactic because Shaner had dated Jeffers' former girlfriend behind his back, and she had ended up pregnant with Shaner's child.

Once again, the case was at a standstill, and Wayne Gulley was till out there, roaming free – and possibly raping and killing again.

#

When Dicks came forth with her confession, most that had been involved in the original case were dumbfounded. But with her fact-by-fact account of the case, her knowledge of certain aspects of the crime that only the killer would have known, the authorities had soon realized that Jeffers had been nothing more than a scapegoat in the case, as well as a pitiful loner just vying for attention.

As far as how many other crimes Gulley may have committed before his capture are concerned, the possibilities could prove to be endless.

There are currently other open murder and rape cases in Indiana, which haven't been solved, some of which at least vaguely resemble Gulley's general description and MO. Whether he was involved in any or all of them is uncertain, and may remain that way, but I personally believe he may have been involved.

For almost three decades, Gulley had all that free time to paint a harmless, respectable picture of himself within our society, all the while committing other crimes. Luckily, over 30 years after the initial horror of it all, justice was finally served for Gibson – but not for Lindy Alton, who had spent all that time reliving the trauma and being burdened with vicious rumors and small town gossip.

Let us keep him in our prayers; fifteen years later, in 1998, he died in a mysterious brush fire.

Gulley received a 50 year sentence, which means he would be 103 years old upon his release.
Let us pray he doesn't live that long.

Wayne Gulley, the weathered face of a heartless, remorseless killer. He thought no more of taking Gibson's life than he would swatting an annoying fly.

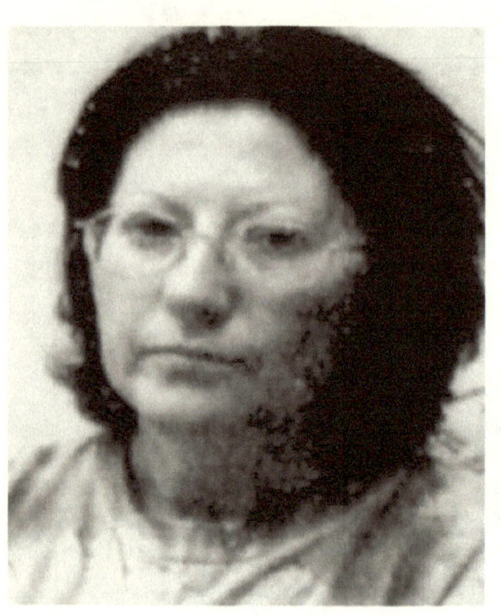

Ella Mae Dicks, Gulley's accomplice in the murder of Sherry Gibson. It was her own vicious stab wounds to Gibson's heart that caused the fatal blow. Let us hope she never sees the light of day again, either.

Hopes and Dreams Shattered
– the Murder of Erika Elaine Norman

He wasn't the most handsome guy in the club, but he had a good personality and he was fun to talk to.

Besides, Erika wasn't the type to judge someone on their outward appearance. She was more interested in a guy that had a good heart and soul. Good looks were just that – looks – and she'd already learned that you couldn't always judge a book by it's cover.

She'd completely captivated Brian from the moment his eyes fell upon her. She'd been at the opposite end of the bar; looking sad and rather bored. Her face was only a pale caricature in the gloom of the bar. But, that warm barroom darkness had done nothing to dim her beauty; if possible it exaggerated it.

At first, he'd told himself to forget it; he'd quietly resigned himself to the fact that it would be another lonely night: frantic and desperate drunken masturbation and morbid sexual fantasies in the emptiness of his one bedroom apartment. This was nothing new; he was used to it, so it didn't bother him too badly. But, still even upon the acceptance of these hard facts he found it difficult, possibly impossible, to take his eyes away from the shadow covered beauty at the opposite end of the bar.

Erika Norman.

He visualized her naked and vulnerable and helpless and dead.

The rest of the night was nothing more than a blur in his mind, until he got her back to her place. She sobered up quick then.

It was much too late to stop his sexual advances by that point. She tried though, even getting into an argument about it with him over his intentions, but he had already decided her fate.

#

On July 4th, 1999, 21-year-old Vincennes University student Erika Elaine Norman simply vanished without a trace.

But not for long.

Two weeks later, a farm worker in Lawrence County Illinois found Norman's decomposing body in a cornfield. When investigators searched her apartment, they found a crime scene that greatly resembled the Brook Baker crime scene in 1997.

However, they soon learned that Norman was last seen in the company of a man named Brian Jones. After being brought in for questioning, he was soon connected to the Baker killing by DNA and charged with her murder.

After Norman's body was found, DNA evidence proved beyond a shadow of a doubt that Jones was involved in her murder as well, and upon realizing there was no use in pleading not guilty, Jones confessed to the second murder in a plea for taking the death penalty off the table, to which Judge Steve Crowley agreed to, stating that Jones "needed to be locked up in an environment where he could receive rehabilitative services." The families of the victims, however, I am sure would have preferred the death penalty.

Jones was sentenced to life in prison without the possibility of parole.

I think he got off too easy.

Erika's beautiful gravestone, to match her beautiful heart and soul.

Brian Jones, a fledgling serial killer who was luckily caught and imprisoned for life before he could fufill any more of his morbid, deadly fantasies any further.

Prince Charming and the Shadow Doll
-The Murder of Kathy Westfall

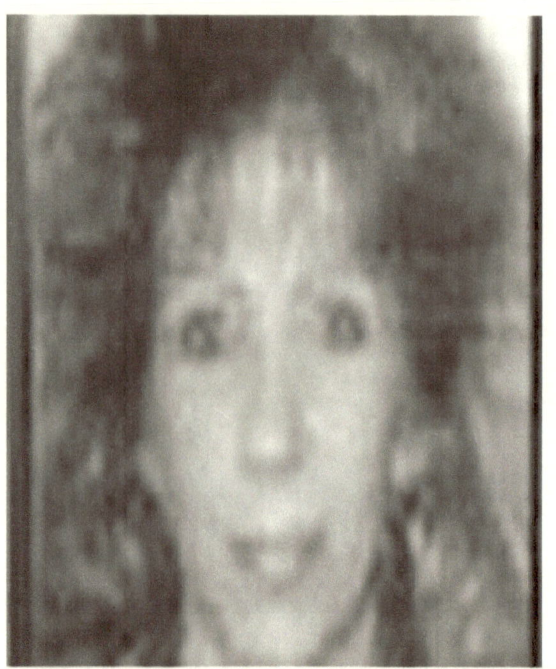

When Kathy comes home at the end of the day there is no one there waiting for her to return. The long shifts at the hospital are taking their toll on her body, heart, and soul.

She switches on the bare bulb that hangs in the kitchenette. The uniform she'd put on just ten hours ago now hangs limply from her exhausted frame. She blinks her heavily made up eyes as she grabs a bottle of wine from the icebox.

She takes a large swallow, grimaces as the cheap wine burns its way down her throat as it lands in her stomach like a lead balloon, exploding into hundreds of tiny little fireballs as it careens into her bloodstream.

She places the cold bottle against her feverish forehead. Behind closed eyes, visions of wide-eyed, thrashing bat wings pulse inside her brain. She opens her weary eyes to see he is there now - the young, handsome man of her dreams - sitting at her table smiling his trademark smile, his ocean-blue eyes twinkling like marbles. In her dreams, he resembles one of her favorite actors - Al Pacino - and she wants to stay within this dream world forever. She feels numb; this is all she ever wanted, this dream to come true; a Prince Charming - her Prince Charming - to come and take her away from all of this sad, lonely existence. Her recent Prince Charming, Brad, hadn't worked out so well.

He stands now, arms outstretched, palms open, inviting her touch. She takes what her offers her, takes it without a second thought, and she instantly feels the world beginning to soften around her. Music begins - she doesn't know where it's coming from, doesn't really care - a soft rock ballad, and she begins to sway to the mildly pulsing beat.

Their faces blur into each other, as one, making shadows on the walls, Prince and Princess Shadow dolls.

"Your heart beats within me," he says, as he leads her by the hand out of the cramped room and outside away from her prison.

The moon's face, fat and full, smiles down upon them, so close she bathes in its light. Suddenly, all goes dark; she is engulfed within the blackness as if it is a death shroud. She can see the bones that hold the very earth together, the lonely, crumbling bones of lovers past in the vortex of loss.

She knows tonight will be no different. She knows that there will be no Prince Charming to save her; he died long, long ago, and only visits her in her dreams.

The numbness wearing off now, she takes what is left of the wine from the table along with a handful of sleeping pills, swallowing five of them, walks into her pitch-black bedroom. As she sleeps she dreams; but not of her Prince Charming, but of this lonely, desolate landscape known as reality.

But the reality of loneliness is better than death.

And death lurked right outside Kathy's door, in the darkness, creeping within the shadows, watching her. The man who was once her Prince Charming was now the Grim Reaper, watching her apartment, peeking in her windows, biding his time, just waiting for the right moment to bring her lonely existence to and end once and for all.

#

Kathleen Westfall was only 44 years old when she was brutally murdered on May 31, 1995.

She was reported missing from work at Good Samaritan Hospital for several days and when police arrived at her apartment around 8:15 pm they found her body. She had been dead at least 48 hours, and had been strangled and beaten to death.

The case quickly went cold, with no leads in the case worth pursuing at the time. Then seven years later, in 2002, an Evansville, Indiana man, Brad Anderson, was arrested and charged with her murder. He was held without bond on charges of murder and being a habitual offender.

Unfortunately for Westfall, Anderson had apparently been a past love interest of hers – and she paid for it with her life.

He was sentenced to 40 years in prison, which means he would be 88 years old when he was eligible for parole.

Kathy never found her Prince Charming, but hopefully she has now found the peace she hadn't found in life.

Brad Anderson, Kathy's Prince Charming – who harbored a deadly intent for her behind those dark eyes.

David Boyer is a Christian, a multi-genre writer, a true crime buff, and the author of several coming of age novellas, numerous horror and scifi stories, as well as the author of numerous essays including the subjects of government corruption, Christianity, bullying, and cyber-stalking.

He lives in Vincennes, Indiana, with his cat, Holly Jean, who now serves as his copy editor by jumping on the computer keyboard when he's not looking.

Books: {Non-fiction}
True crime:
Small Town Murder: True Crime Stories From Knox County, Indiana
Murder In the Hoosier Heartland: Infamous Indiana Murderers & Fledgling Serial Killers
Murder & Mayhem In the Hoosier Heartland: Mysterious Disappearances & Bizarre Murders In Indiana
The Blitz: A Rape Victim's Story
Vanished In Vincennes: the Mysterious Disappearance and Death Of Dolores Oliver
47 Years of Hell: The Dolores Oliver Murder: Still Unsolved
Small Town Murder In Knox County, Indiana: Hate Crimes, Witch Hunts, and A Definitive List of Indiana Serial Killers
The Guy In The Blue Shirt

Non-fiction: {paranormal, bio & memoir}
Haunted Heartland: Haunted Hoosiers Tell Their Ghost Stories
Strange Happenings In the Hoosier Heartland
I Remember When, In Vincennes...Volume 1
Growing Up In Vincennes – Volumes 2 – 5
The Time of Our Lives: Growing Up Cool In Vincennes, Indiana

Essays:
Bullying: the Road to Recovery and Forgiveness
Privacy In the Age of the Internet: How Sexting and Sharing Private Photos Can lead To Cyber-Stalking

Once An Alcoholic, Always An Alcoholic? The Cold Hard Truth About Our Addictions
Travesties of Jutice: Flaws In Our Legal System That Imprison the Innocent
Will the REAL Christian Please Stand Up?
Racism in the 21st Century: ALL Lives Matter
Conflicted Souls: How the Man In Black Saved My Life
Crossing the Rainbow Bridge: Saying Goodbye To Our Beloved Pets

Books: {Fiction}
Mystery, Indiana
Human Sawdust

Stories: {Long fiction, novellas}
Mystery, Indiana
The Mind of Luther Biggs
LUTHER
Jenny
Lester Talbot and His Magic Eye
Beautiful Ghosts
Pretty Flamingo
Jack and Norma Jean
The Things We Leave Behind – Volumes 1 – 3
Ghosts of Summer
Gardens
Claustrophobia
The Cemetery Artist
Brain Pie
Beast
The Jailhouse Movie Star
Easy Pickings
The Dominant Thumb
Joyride
The Maverick
Freak
Grandma's Gooseberry Pie
Dancing With the King

Always In My Heart
Hillbilly Moonshine Zombies
Home
Sheva
A Debt Repaid In Full
The Enlightening Darkness
The Good Neighbor
Wander
The Hungry Ones
A Gunfighter's Legacy
Dead Man's Hand
Inhuman Experiments – Part 1, 2, and 3
Jennifer
Spider Bait

Short stories {Comic, dark humor}
Zipper Head
The Big Brown Banana Express
Uncle Marty

Bonus:
Excerpt from the book
Vanished In the Hoosier Heartland:
Unsolved Missing Person Cases In Indiana

For those who are still missing:
You have not been forgotten, and never will be.

Missing in the darkness,
vanished without a trace,
with only the memories and photographs,
to fill an empty place.
Frequent prayer and fervent cries,
is there anyone there?
But the only sound
was the silent eternal fanfare.

For a long time
its deafening sound
subdued by a path
through lost and found.

Laughter and sorrow,
anguish and grief,
all the moments of a life
but with no relief.

Everything and nothing
one within and between all,
gentle, loving, pervading,
the eternal silence falls.

Introduction

After spending the last several years conducting a lot of research into missing persons cases, I have come to the conclusion that regardless of what evidence – or lack thereof – exists at the time, a lot of these missing people have been the victims of a serial killer.

As with a lot of missing person's cases, a majority of these disappearances have absolutely no logical explanation. This man was happy with his job, happy with his life, and was making good money and owned a nice car and had a lot of close friends. This woman was engaged to be married to the man of her dreams and looking forward to their life together.

Which brings to mind my belief that a lot of missing persons cases have to do with the "roaming serial killer" theory, in which a serial killer just happens to be roaming through that specific area at the time on their way to somewhere else, always moving along to avoid capture, and just happened upon the victim in question by circumstance.

Then, upon seeing a perfect opportunity to claim another victim – an isolated area around daylight or dusk, with no other witnesses in sight – the killer takes advantage of the situation and performs what I refer to as a "quick grab and run," abducting the victim quietly and quickly, and by the time the victim has been listed as missing, they have already been murdered, dumped, and their killer long since gone.

Take, for example, infamous serial killer Henry lee Lucas, who, by his own admittance, along with his cannibal killer buddy Ottis Toole, killed almost 300 people from 1977 to 1983, including Adam Walsh, son of famed *America's Most Wanted* host John Walsh.

The reason they eluded capture for so many years? It was simple enough for the seasoned drifter; they never *stayed* in one place too long.

In addition, roaming serial killers also tend to change their MO on a regular basis. For example; if they kill one victim by strangulation? The next one will be shot with a gun or stabbed with a knife or tossed off a bridge, and so on. Their MO will change as often as their current location.

Some roaming serial killers even dispose of some victims by eating part of their remains. Cannibalistic killer Ottis Toole, also known as "the cannibal kid," was known to have disposed of some his victims remains by carving up their body, disposing of some of it in a wooded area where he knew the local wildlife would drag it away, and use the rest of it to roast over and open fire, barbecue style, complete with his own special barbecue sauce recipe, made with human blood.

Therefore, even if he was captured and arrested on suspicion of murder, there would be no hard evidence on which to base a conviction.

The roaming or "drifting" serial killer can remain at large for as long as two decades, as long as they keep changing up their game. That is why, to me, it is more than obvious that at least a small – if not more – percentage of missing persons who had absolutely no reason to just up and disappear were most likely victims of serial killers.

They say that the truth is always stranger than fiction, and that often times the obvious reasons for someone's disappearance is in all actuality the *least* likely reason for their disappearance.

As far as at least some of the case profiles in this book are concerned, I tend to agree.

David Boyer / September, 2023

A Drug Overdose That Led To A Cover Up?
The Mysterious Disappearance
Of Lauren Spierer

Name: Lauren Spierer
Description:
Blonde hair
Blue eyes
Height: 4 feet 11 inches tall
Weight: 90 pounds
Last seen on June 3, 2011, Bloomington, Indiana

Case details:

When Rob and Charlene Spierer dropped their daughter, Lauren, off at Indiana University in 2009, they felt she was in a safe place, had nothing at all to worry about. But what they didn't know was Bloomington had it's dark side, a underground culture of booze and drugs and a totally carefree and careless lifestyle – which, unknown to them, Lauren had become a part of.

To make matters worse, Lauren had been arrested for public intoxication about nine months before she vanished, and after her disappearance, police found a small amount of cocaine in her dorm room. Charlene was astonished at the news, finding it hard to believe that her daughter would take part in such illegal and unhealthy activities.

However, police believe that Lauren's probable impairment led to her disappearance – and possible demise – because under the influence of drugs and alcohol, she wasn't able to fend off her assailant. Sad, but true, in so many deaths and disappearances.

Lauren had been dating her high school boyfriend and fellow Indiana University student Jesse Wolfe up until her disappearance, but the night she vanished, she had been out for a night of wild partying with another student she had just met that night, a young man named Corey Rossman. Another student, Seth Parker, told police that Rossman told him much later that he and Lauren had been 'pre-gaming' at another student's place before heading off to Kilroy's Sports bar close by around 2 am.

Police learned that Lauren was at Kilroy's for only about half an hour before she had already removed her shoes and socks and leaving them and her cellphone behind when she left, a clear indication of how intoxicated she was by that point.

Shortly thereafter, Lauren and Rossman left and walked back to her off campus apartment, where they were accosted by four other male students, who apparently didn't like the way Rossman was 'handling' Lauren in the hallway. Rossman became smart aleck with one of them, upon which time the other man punched Rossman in the face, knocking him down. At that point in the altercation Lauren and Rossman fled on foot back to his place not too far away.

Shortly thereafter, a security camera shows Lauren stumbling over her own feet and Rossman flinging her over his shoulder to carry her the rest of the way. Once they arrived at his place, he became sick to his stomach and passed out. Not wanting the responsibility of two drunks, Rossman's roommate took Lauren next door to a friend's apartment, Jason Rosenbaum.

Jason suggested that she lie down on the couch and sleep it off, but Lauren was adamant about staying up longer and wanting to party. Not wanting the responsibility either, Jason then suggested that if she didn't want to sleep it off, she could go party somewhere else. The last time he saw Lauren, she was stumbling down the street, very intoxicated and unsteady on her feet.

He was the last person to see her before she vanished.

#

The next evening, as Rob and Charlene sat down to their normal family dinner, the phone rang and they received the heart-stopping news that their daughter was missing.

In no time at all, Charlene and Rob found themselves in front of news cameras, talking to the world about their missing daughter. Hundreds of volunteers turned out to help them launch a massive search for Lauren, even going as far as to search a local landfill nearby, but with no results.

Lauren had seemed to have vanished into thin air.

"I start my everyday hoping that today is the day. I go to sleep every night knowing that I have failed and that I haven't done enough," an emotional Charlene said at the time.

Five years later the missing posters are all but gone around the Bloomington campus. But the Spierers have not given up and quietly, behind the scenes, the case is very much alive as Garrett and the team of private investigators have turned up new witnesses, leads and theories.

#

Investigators started with Lauren's closest associates and the men she was with that night, knowing from experience that when something like this happened, it more often than not involved someone within their own social circle.

Almost immediately, odd behavior from the men involved made authorities suspicious. For example, both men Lauren had been with that night hired lawyers to represent them. If they were innocent of any involvement, why lawyer up?

Then Lauren's long time boyfriend, Jesse Wolfe, whom had even helped with the search for Lauren, stopped cold, not having any contact with the family at all. Upon being questioned, he told police he was at home watching the NBA playoffs that night, alone, and went to bed around 2am – which, coincidentally, was around the same time she vanished.

However, his roommate told police Jesse was home all night, and never left the apartment for anything. Other friends stepped up to vouch for him too, saying that he was a very loving boyfriend to Lauren, and would never harm her in any way.

When Rossman was interrogated – and even submitted a DNA sample – he told police that he was not the last person who'd seen her, and he was hoping and praying for her and her family. He also said that he had 'blacked out' after being punched in the head, and doesn't remember anything until the next day after sobering up.

Rob Spierer, however, doesn't believe him. It was

hard for him to swallow that a healthy, strapping young man like Rossman would suffer from complete memory loss from one punch to the head.

"I think it's a case of self-preservation. Understandable human condition," Rob said. "I'm not sure of anything, but what I do know is that there's been a complete lack of cooperation. And he was the person who spent the most time with Lauren in the last hours of her being seen."

Rossman did, however, continue to be cooperative with the authorities.

#

Another theory was that maybe a drifter, possibly a nomadic serial killer, was passing through Bloomington at the time and, noticing Lauren stumbling down the street, and marked her as an easy target for an abduction. On the night Lauren disappeared, police said a white truck was spotted on surveillance footage not far from where she was last seen.

Then the police learned that ex-convict James McClish, a man who had been in prison again for spousal abuse, had recently been paroled from prison, and was living in a half-way house only ten minutes away from where Lauren had vanished.

Then, a woman from McClish's past reached out to the police and said, "You need to check this guy out. I know damn well he was there. He told me that if I didn't want the same thing to happen to me that happened to her {Lauren} I better not piss him off, give him any bullshit."

The woman went as far as to tell police McClish

had raped and killed Lauren, and buried her remains on a farm in Southern Indiana.

When approached about Lauren's disappearance, McClish denied any involvement and even agreed to take a lie detector test, which he passed with flying colors.

#

The next theory pertained to Robert Strange, aka "Bo Dean," a member of a local biker gang known as the "Sons of Silence."

Police theorized that since Lauren was into the drug culture, and Strange was known as a violent "enforcer" for the gang, maybe she owed him money for drugs and couldn't pay him, so he killed her and dumped her body where it wouldn't be found. Strange had even been known to brag that "dead bodies made good fertilizer."

Upon being approached at his home by police – as well as a news crew for the ABC TV show, "20/20," he wouldn't even step outside, shielding his face from the camera and saying, "I had nothing to do with it. I don't even know the broad. I told you that... There ain't no body here [and] I ain't never seen the broad. Never been around her."

Upon further investigation, based on Lauren's cell phone records, it was unlikely she had suspicious links to Indianapolis, where she was supposedly taken. Strange was looking less like a suspect and more like someone with enemies trying to make trouble for him by implicating him in Lauren's disappearance.

Just another dead end.

#

As Lauren's parents grew frustrated with the lack of results, they also grew frustrated with the local police in Bloomington.

Rob said, "It seemed like they were bound and determined *not* to keep us in the loop as to what they'd found, where the investigation was going. It was almost like they were trying to shut us out altogether."

To make matters even more frustrating for her parents, the police literally *refused* to release additional surveillance footage of Lauren from the night of June 2 and morning of June 3. The move baffled Rob and Charlene, as many police stations publicize as much information as possible.

In their frustration, they hired a private investigator, Beau Dietl, and set up a web site to collect more tips as to what may have happened to Lauren. It was through this web site they received a tip that a man currently serving time in an Indiana prison may have had information about Lauren's death.

The story goes as follows: the inmate, Corey Hamersley, was sitting with other inmates playing cards when when Lauren's photo came up on the television mounted to the wall. It is said that upon seeing her photo, Hamersly said, "Oh man...I know the guys that did that to her. She was at a party with a bunch of college geeks, getting drunk and doing ecstasy. She OD'd, and they took her body down to the Ohio River and dumped her off."

It was a very simple scenario compared to the others, which is why the police had finally taken one of the theories to heart. In their experience, no matter how many wild and complicated scenarios they could come up with during an investigation, sometimes, it was the most simple one that rang true.

That theory, along with Rob and Charlene having told police that Lauren had a heart condition, made police believe that Lauren, under the influence of too much alcohol and drugs, had a fatal heart attack, and in a blind panic, some of the male students present had taken her body to the river and tossed her in, believing she would never be found.

"Now it's just all about finding her, getting answers to what happened to her," Rob Spierer said. "We know that she just didn't fall off the face of the earth and vaporize. Something happened to our daughter, and we believe that there are people out there that know exactly what happened to our daughter."

Charlene readily agreed, saying, "That's the most frustrating thing, knowing that somebody knows right now. And they could change our lives in the blink of an eye. Please...just tell us *where* Lauren is."

Anyone with any relevant information about Lauren is urged to call the Bloomington police department, call the HelpFindLauren.com tip line at 1-812-339-4477, or send an email to helpfindlauren {at} gmail.com.